i ♥ macarons

i ♥ macarons

By Hisako Ogita

CHRONICLE BOOKS

SAN FRANCISCO

First English edition published in the United States of America
in 2009 by Chronicle Books LLC.
First published in Japan in 2006 by Shufu-To-Seikatsusha.

Library of Congress Cataloging-in-Publication Data available.

ISBN 9780-8118-6871-6

Manufactured in China

I Love Macarons
Editors: Junko Satoh, Seiji Yamamura
Planning and research: Mitsuko Kohashi
Photography: Yasuo Nagumo, David Barich
English translation: Alma Reyes and Seishi Maruyama
Art Direction and design: Mika Takaichi, David Barich
Stylist: Akiko Suzuki
Cooking assistant: Mari Watanabe
Production: David Barich, Rico Komanoya (ricorico)

English Translation rights arranged with Shufu-To-Seikatsusha
through Timo Associates Inc., Tokyo

10 9 8 7 6 5 4

Chronicle Books LLC
680 Second Street
San Francisco, California 94107
www.chroniclebooks.com

Notes on the ingredients, utensils, and other equipment:

* One tablespoon = 0.5 ounce/15 milliliters
* One teaspoon = 0.2 ounce/5 milliliters
* One cup = 6.8 ounces/200 milliliters
* Use medium-size eggs.
* A 1,500 = watt toaster oven can be used to bake macarons.
* The baking time varies depending on the heat source condition
  and the model of the oven. Adjust the baking time while checking
  the pastry based on the time indicated in the recipes.

CONTENTS

Macarons. Their white, pink, yellow, green, and various other color combinations and their round, domelike shape make them charming. The sweet, crispy texture of the puffs and the thick cream between them add a rich harmony to this delicate pastry. It is the type of pastry that makes you so happy when you receive it as a gift that you are bound to say, "Wow, how cute they are!"

Several years ago, macarons may not have been popular in many countries. They were often placed in corners of pastry shops' display shelves. Now, macarons are popular. One can find many lovely macaron shops or buy these pastries in coffee shops. In some shops, macarons are displayed on the top shelf counters, as if to show off the skill of their bakers.

In this book, I have tried to create some recipes for making superb macarons at home. After going through many trials—such as trying to figure out how to make the pied (the little foot of the macaron) or how not to crack the pastries—I finally came up with recipes that anyone can make. I also used ordinary equipment and utensils for preparing the ingredients, such as simple cookware and a regular oven, so that anyone can give the recipes a try.

When you start making macarons, you might fail several times, but don't give up! You will certainly be successful when you learn the secrets for mixing the paste, knowing the timing for drying, mastering the characteristics of the oven, and more. These small and cute macarons have a variety of flavors and colors that make them perfect as gifts. For that reason, I have also presented some ideas for easy gift wrapping. I hope you enjoy macarons not only at teatime but also on Christmas, Valentine's Day, and other special occasions.

—Hisako Ogita

THE THREE MAJOR INGREDIENTS FOR MAKING MACARONS:
GROUND ALMONDS, POWDERED SUGAR, AND EGG WHITES

CRISPY CRUST!

SOFT AND MOIST FILLING

CUTE PASTRY SHAPES

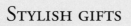

STYLISH GIFTS

WHICH ONE DO YOU LIKE BEST?

DELICIOUS TOPPINGS

Part 1

MAKING MACARON BATTER

There are two methods for making macaron batter, and each produces a different texture. The most common method is to make meringue first and then mix it with almond powder. The other method is to mix Italian meringue and almond powder. This book also presents two methods for coloring and flavoring the batter. One method calls for adding the colors or flavors to the almond powder; the other method is to add them to the meringue.

MAJOR INGREDIENTS FOR MAKING MACARON BATTER

You will need ground almonds, powdered sugar, and flavorings that do not contain cornstarch. Pay attention to the ingredients on the package when you buy powdered flavorings because the powder that contains cornstarch does not work well for making the macaron batter.

Egg whites

Bring eggs to room temperature. Eggs at room temperature beat up better than an egg that you crack open right from the refrigerator. It is fine to use frozen egg whites after thawing them.

Ground almonds or almond flour or meal

You can buy almond meal or flour at many supermarkets or mail-order sources. Be sure to store almond flour in the freezer, as it goes rancid quickly. You can also buy whole or sliced almonds and grind them finely for an excellent effect.

Powdered sugar

Use pure powdered sugar or sugar that contains oligosaccharide. Just as with almond powder, avoid using powdered sugar that contains cornstarch because it may cause the pastry to crack.

Other ingredients

Powdered or cube flavoring that contains little moisture (hazelnut, dried raspberry, etc.) is mixed with almond powder, whereas flavoring with moisture (natural colorings and food colorings dissolved in water) is mixed with meringue.

Equipment and Utensils for Making the Batter

You don't need any special cookware for making macarons, though an electric hand mixer or a stand mixer can be useful for power when beating the egg whites. A heat-resistant spatula is also recommended. You will need two trays for baking the macarons. For the recipes in this book, I used a baking tray 12 by 12 inches (31 by 31 centimeters).

Strainer

This is used for sifting the flour. Sift the flour quickly and evenly by shaking the strainer and stirring the nut/sugar mixture with your fingertips.

Baking mats

I recommend using baking mats to line the baking sheet when making macarons. You may use regular parchment paper, but baking mats, such as Silpat and other nonstick baking mats, can be used many times since they are washable.

Measuring cup

You may use this for making the batter with Italian meringue. A heat-resistant cup is recommended.

Mixing bowl

This is used for mixing first the meringue and then the batter. A deep stainless-steel bowl is the best type to use because it conducts heat well.

Kitchen scale

The first step for successful dessert making is to measure the ingredients accurately with a scale. A digital scale is recommended if you plan to buy a new scale.

Pastry bag and tip

Pastry bags can be made of either a soft or hard material, with a pattern on the tip. In this book, a metal tip with a 0.4-inch (1-centimeter) opening was used for making a macaron about 0.9 inch (2.5 centimeters) in size.

Hand mixer

There are various types of mixers. In a five-speed mixer, which was used in this book, speed 5 corresponds to fast; speed 3 corresponds to medium; and speed 1 corresponds to slow.

Spatula

This is used for mixing the batter and scooping it into a pastry bag. A spatula with a flexible tip is the best type.

How to Make Basic Macaron Batter (Vanilla Flavor)

Macaron batter is made by mixing ground almonds and meringue, but you can make various types of meringue, depending on the ingredients you use. These steps show you the process for making regular meringue (called French meringue) by whisking egg whites while gradually adding sugar.

Ingredients (makes about 2 dozen macarons)

⅔ cup (3 ounces/85 grams) ground almonds
1½ cups (5.25 ounces/150 grams) powdered sugar
3 large egg whites, at room temperature
5 tablespoons/65 grams granulated sugar
1 teaspoon vanilla extract, or seeds from ½ vanilla bean

1.

Cut a sheet of parchment paper (or other nonstick liner) to fit your baking sheet. Draw 1-inch (2.5-centimeter) circles on the paper, spacing them at least ½ inch (1.5 centimeters) apart. This pattern will be your guide for squeezing out the macaron batter.

2.

In a food processor, grind almonds and powdered sugar together to a fine powder. Sift the mixture through a medium-mesh sieve twice. Set aside.

Pointer:

Before beating the mixture in step 3 with a hand mixer, scrape the remaining meringue from the bowl's sides with a spatula. Do this each time you start the mixer.

Pointer:

After the sugar has been added, beat egg whites on high speed until they reach stiff, glossy peaks, about one minute. You can use a hand mixer or a stand mixer.

3.

In a stainless-steel mixing bowl, beat egg whites on high speed until they are foamy. Gradually add the granulated sugar to the egg whites, as shown.

4.

Add vanilla and stir lightly.

Note:

If you are using a vanilla bean, to take out the seeds, slit the pod and scrape out the seeds.

5.

When the meringue is stiff, firm, and has a glossy texture, it is done.

CONTINUED ON PAGE 26

6.

Add half of the sifted flour mixture from step 2. Stir it with a spatula while scooping it up from the bottom of the bowl.

7.

Add the rest of the flour and mix it lightly in a circular motion.

Macaronnage = term for mixing flour and meringue to make macarons

Macaronner = term for mixing the batter until it is firm and drips slowly when it is scooped out.

8.

Macaronnage
When you run out of flour, press and spread out the batter against the bowl's sides. Scoop the batter from the bottom and turn it upside down (see photo at bottom, second from left). Repeat this process about 15 times.

Pointer:

If the macaronnage step is repeated less than 10 times, the baked macarons will lack luster. However, when it is repeated more than 20 times, oil stains may remain on the pastry's surface when the macarons are baked.

9.

Macaronner
When the batter becomes nicely firm and drips slowly as you scoop it with a spatula, the mixture is done.

10.

Attach a 0.4-inch (1.01 centimeter) tip to the pastry bag. Twist the bag to hold the tip tightly. This prevents the batter from leaking out.

11.

Place the pastry bag, tip down, inside a deep measuring cup and pour the batter made in step 9 into it.

12.

After pouring the batter into the bag, clip the bag top to prevent the batter from coming out. You can use a string or rubber band, as well as a clip, to close it.

13.

Place the sheet used in step 1 on the baking sheet and squeeze out the batter onto the center of the circles. Make small circles since the batter tends to spread out after being squeezed.

14.

Rap the baking sheet firmly against the counter or other flat surface. This helps the macarons hold their rounded shape and helps the *pied,* or little "foot," to form.

15.

Dry the batter at room temperature, uncovered, for 15 minutes. A slight crust should form on top of the macarons. On rainy days, it helps to dehumidify the room.

16.

If the batter circles do not stick to your finger when you touch them, the drying process is complete. On a dry and sunny day, the drying process takes approximately 30 minutes.

Pointer:

The batter is settled when no tips can be seen in the circles.

BAKING THE MACARONS

1.

Place oven racks in the center of the oven. Preheat the oven to 375°F (190°C).

2.

Stack the baking sheet with the batter circles into an empty baking sheet and slide both into the oven.

3.

Bake for 15 to 18 minutes, until slightly crisp and crackled on top.

4.

To bake the macarons evenly, rotate the tray so that macarons at the rear come up front and vice versa.

WHY USE TWO TRAYS?

Using two trays, one inside the other, prevents the bottom of the macarons from getting overbaked. Using two trays is also effective for preventing macarons from puffing up too much or cracking.

PIED

As macarons bake, small pleatlike frills form at the bottom of each. This pleat is called a *pied,* or foot. Without it, the pastry cannot be called a macaron. Some bakers attribute the pied to the macaronnage, some to the oven temperature, and some to a good rap of the baking sheet on the counter before baking.

5.

If the insides of the macarons are still soft after 15 minutes, lower oven temperature to 300°F (150°C), cover the tray with aluminum foil, and bake for another 2 to 3 minutes.

6.

The macarons are done! Remove the baking sheet from the oven and cool on a wire rack. When the macarons are completely cooled, remove them from the baking sheet.

* Spread cream (see recipes on pages 42 to 53) between two of the macaron shells, and they are ready to be eaten!

Pointer:

Macarons can be kept in the refrigerator for about one week if you keep them in a sealed container.

How to Make Macarons with Italian Meringue

This recipe is for making macarons with Italian meringue by using egg whites whipped until they are firm and adding syrup boiled to soft-ball stage 240°F (115°C). Hot syrup sterilizes the meringue, which keeps it well preserved. The bubbles are also kept intact, and the surface of the macarons is crunchy.

Ingredients (makes about 2 dozen macarons)

2 tablespoons water
5 tablespoons/65 grams granulated sugar
⅔ cup (3 ounces/85 grams) ground almonds or almond meal
1½ cups (5.25 ounces/150 grams) powdered sugar
3 large egg whites, at room temperature
1 teaspoon vanilla extract, or seeds from ½ vanilla bean

1.

Combine water and granulated sugar in a small saucepan. Stir to combine.

Note:

Mix ground almonds and powdered sugar, sift them twice, and set aside.

2.

Place a saucepan over medium-high heat and bring the sugar-water syrup to a boil. Do not stir; rather, swirl the pan. You may also wash down the sugar crystals on the side of the pan with a brush dipped in water. Bring the syrup to 235°F to 240°F, soft-ball stage.

Pointer:

You can also heat the syrup in a microwave. Heat for 1 minute, stir to dissolve sugar, and return to oven for 4 more minutes. Be careful with the hot container.

3.

In a mixing bowl or the bowl of a stand mixer, beat egg whites at high speed for about 30 seconds.

4.

To test the syrup, drip a small bead into a small bowl of water. Check if the syrup is sticky enough (like corn syrup) so that you can pick up and make a ball with using your fingers. If it is not sticky enough, heat a bit longer.

Pointer:

Place a wet cloth under the bowl to stabilize it so it does not move when you beat the meringue.

5.

Beat the egg whites used in step 3 entirely with a hand mixer while pouring the syrup into the bowl in a fine stream, as done in step 4, as though you were hanging a piece of thread. Keep beating at medium or slow speed until the mixture feels cool when you touch the bottom of the bowl.

6.

Beat until the meringue is firm and smooth. To complete the recipe, follow steps 6 to 16 as illustrated on pages 26 to 27.

Adding Flavor to the Macaron Batter

You can add flavor to the macaron batter in two ways. One method is to mix a flavoring ingredient with the almond powder, and the other method is to mix it with the meringue. A flavor with a little moisture can be mixed with almond powder. A food coloring dissolved in water and other colorings with some moisture can be mixed in meringue. In this way, the taste and fragrance will not be too strong. Enjoy these soft flavors.

Macarons with flavoring ingredients mixed into the almond powder

You use flavoring ingredients by mixing them with almond powder and powdered sugar. (See step 2 on page 24.) The ingredients and processes to create other flavors are the same.

Cinnamon

1 teaspoon (0.20 ounce/5 grams) cinnamon
⅔ cup (3 ounce/85 grams) almond power
1½ cups, (5.25 ounces/150 grams) powdered su

Framboise (raspberry)

2 tablespoons (0.75 ounce/30 grams) dried raspberries, ground in a food processor
⅔ cup (3 ounces/85 grams) almond powder
1½ cups (5.25 ounces/150 grams) powdered sugar

Sesame

2 tablespoons (1 ounce/30 grams) ground sesame seeds
⅔ cup (3 ounces/85 grams) almond powder
1½ cups, (5.25 ounces/150 grams) powdered sugar

Caramel

2 tablespoons (1 ounce/30 grams) caramel powder
⅔ cup (3 ounces/85 grams) almond powder
1½ cups, (5.25 ounces/150 grams) powdered suga

Hazelnut

1 teaspoon (0.20 ounces/5 grams) hazelnut powde
⅔ cup (3 ounces/85 grams) almond powder
1½ cups, (5.25 ounces/150 grams) powdered suga

Chocolate

3 tablespoons (1 ounce/25 grams) Dutch-processed cocoa powder
½ cup (1.75 ounces/50 grams) almond powder
1 cup, (1.75 ounces/50 grams) powdered sugar

Coconut

2 tablespoons (1 ounce/30 grams) dry coconut powder
⅔ cup (3 ounces/85 grams) almond powder
1½ cups, (5.25 ounces/150 grams) powdered sugar

Purple Yam

2 tablespoons (1 ounce/30 grams) purple yam powder

 ⅔ cup (3 ounces/85 grams) almond powder

1½ cups (5.25 ounces/150 grams) powdered sugar

Pistachio

 ⅓ cup (1 ½ ounces/45 grams) pistachios, ground in a food processor

⅔ cup (3 ounces/85 grams) almond powder

1½ cups, (5.25 ounces/150 grams) powdered sugar

Matcha (green tea)

1 teaspoon matcha

⅔ cup (3 ounces/85 grams) almond powder

1½ cups (5.25 ounces/150 grams) powdered sugar

Pumpkin

 1 teaspoon pumpkin powder

⅔ cup (3 ounces/85 grams) almond powder

1½ cups (5.25 ounces/150 grams) powdered sugar

Black tea

1 teaspoon finely ground black tea powder

⅔ cup (3 ounces/85 grams) almond powder

1½ cups (5.25 ounces/150 grams) powdered sugar

Café

2 teaspoons instant coffee, finely ground in a food processor

⅔ cup (3 ounces/85 grams) almond powder

1½ cups (5.25 ounces/150 grams) powdered sugar

Kinako (roasted soybean flour)

 1 teaspoon (0.20 ounce/5 grams) kinako

⅔ cup (3 ounces/85 grams) almond powder

1½ cups (5.25 ounces/150 grams) powdered sugar

MACARONS WITH FLAVORING INGREDIENTS
MIXED WITH MERINGUE

Refer to How to Use Food Coloring on page 35 to learn how to add flavoring ingredients after you have made meringue, as illustrated in step 5 on page 25. If you mix the meringue too much with the flavoring ingredient, it becomes too hard, so stop mixing when the colors and flavors have spread thoroughly. When you add a flavor to Italian meringue, mix it when the meringue has cooled down after adding syrup. (Refer to step 5 on page 31.) Enjoy the bright colors of these macarons.

Cassis (black currant)
Red and blue food coloring

Mint
1 tablespoon dried mint
Green food coloring
4 tablespoons (2 ounces/60 grams) almond powder
4 tablespoons (2 ounces/60 grams) powdered sugar

Rose
1 teaspoon rose water
Red food coloring

Red
More red food coloring than for the rose flavor

Blue
Blue food coloring

Yellow-green
Yellow and green food coloring

Caramel
½ tablespoon caramel coloring

Yellow
Yellow food coloring

Orange
½ teaspoon orange flower water
Red and yellow food coloring

Toppings are fun to use!

You can sprinkle some toppings on the macarons after squeezing out macaron batter and leveling it. (See step 14 on page 27.) The toppings should not melt when you bake the macarons.

Chocolate with Cacoa Nibs
Sprinkle some cacoa nibs on a chocolate macaron. You can also use toasted minced walnut.

Vanilla with Black Pepper
Sprinkle some black pepper on a vanilla macaron.

Pistachio with Pistachio
Top a pistachio macaron with ground pistachios.

Framboise with Framboise (raspberry)
Sprinkle minced dried framboise on a framboise macaron.

Mint with Mint
Sprinkle dried mint on a mint macaron.

How to use food coloring

1.

Put food coloring in a small bowl and add a small amount of water, dissolving the added color with a spoon.

2.

Gradually add the coloring from step 1 into the meringue; stir quickly but not too much.

3.

The color becomes lighter after it is baked, so make a little darker batter.

Yellow with Cocoa
Sprinkle cocoa powder on a yellow macaron.

WHEN YOU CANNOT MAKE A GOOD MACARON

Macarons are small and cute. But their beautiful shapes are difficult to make, for both beginners and those who have tried making them many times. There are several causes for failure, but most of the time, it depends on what happens to the macarons in the oven. When you try making them again, try out some of the baking pointers—first, at a high temperature, then at a low temperature—or try not to let steam form inside the oven. When you get used to these pointers, you should be able to make beautiful macarons that will surprise everyone around you. Don't give up!

WHEN THE MACARON CRACKS . . .

Possible causes

1. You baked without drying the surface of the macaron.

2. You did not use two oven trays when baking.

3. The oven was too hot, and the bottom of the baking sheet got too much heat.

Note:

The room temperature, heated area, air circulation, and the way steam escapes differ depending on the type of oven used and its internal size. Try making the macaron again while checking to correct each cause mentioned above.

WHEN THE MACARONS ARE NOT GLOSSY . . .

Possible cause

1. Insufficient macaronnage (See page 26.)

Note:

Try mixing the macaron mixture 15 times for macaronnage. The amount of mixing varies, depending on your strength and the stiffness of the meringue. Mix until the mixture is hard enough to drop from a spatula. Then, slowly scoop out the paste. It should look a little sticky when it spreads.

WHEN YOU CANNOT MAKE A PIED . . .

Possible cause

1. You have dried the mixture too much. (It is too dry if it feels hard. If the paste filling is dry, the pied cannot be formed correctly.)

Note:

The length of drying time for macarons varies from season to season. Try to set your air conditioner at "dry" mode or use an electric fan on a humid day in order to quicken the drying process and create a smooth texture.

WHEN YOU SEE OIL STAINS . . .

Possible causes

1. You used old almond meal.

2. You used ground almonds exposed for a long time at room temperature.

3. You did not bake them long enough.

4. You mixed too much during macaronnage.

Note:

Leave the mixture of almond powder and powdered sugar in the refrigerator before mixing it with meringue.

Macarons Parisien Style

Macarons are typically known as traditional French pastries, but it is said that they originally came from Italy. In the mid-sixteenth century, when Catherine de' Medici, daughter of the noble duke of Florence, Lorenzo II de' Medici, married the French King Henry II, she brought her cooks and bakers along to France and introduced a variety of pastries to the French people. The macaron was one of them.

Since then, macarons have become very popular in France and different versions had been perfected in each region. In the region of Lorraine, you will find "Nancy macarons" that have a cracked surface and do not use meringue. In Bordeaux, wine is added to the "Saint-Émilion macarons." In Paris, you'll find *"macaron parisien"* that has a smooth, plump surface. This is one of the most well-known types of macarons presented in this book.

Currently, there are countless types of macarons, and you will see top pâtissiers boasting their skills in Parisian pastry shops. Mari Watanabe, a pastry chef friend of mine who lives in France, came back to Japan to help me photograph macarons. Her baking skills were appreciated by a French pastry shop, and she now makes "Mari's Macarons." She says that the latest fad in macarons uses marble patterns. She brought home some French powder and made trendy macarons for me.

Part 2

MAKING THE CREAM FILLING

When you finish making the macaron batter, you can make the cream filling. This book presents two types of butter cream, custard cream, ganache, lemon curd, caramel cream, and others. You can also use jam and red bean paste, which can be purchased at many Asian stores. Let's make a variety of cream fillings to expand our flavor rainbow!

MAJOR UTENSILS FOR MAKING THE CREAM

You have a variety of choices when it comes to kitchen utensils, depending on the types of cream you are making. Utensils that are easy to handle and generally useful are the key to proper baking. I recommend stainless-steel bowls and square pans because these conduct heat quickly.

Measuring instruments

You will need a digital scale and measuring spoons. It is important to measure the ingredients accurately as the recipe instructs you. A tablespoon measures 0.5 ounce/15 milliliters, while a teaspoon measures 0.2 ounce/5 milliliters. Scoop an ingredient up with a spoon and then level the surface with a knife or other tool.

Whisk

This is used for mixing ingredients. A small whisk is useful for making lemon curd. Use a whisk that has a thick wire and a firm grip.

Strainer and mixing bowl

A strainer is used when adding tea and other liquids to thin the cream. A mixing bowl is used to stir the cream. A deep bowl is good for preventing the cream from spattering when it is whipped.

Spatula

This is used to mix butter and cream. You may stir ingredients while heating them up. In this case, a heat-resistant spatula with a certain degree of flexibility is recommended.

Tea strainer

This is used when you sprinkle cocoa powder or powdered sugar on macarons. Tap it lightly with your fingers to sprinkle the powder evenly.

Saucepan

This is used to warm milk and whipping cream or to make caramel cream.

Square pan

In this pan, you can spread out the custard cream. You may have to cool it down quickly, so a stainless-steel tray is desirable because it conducts heat well.

Hand mixer

This is used to beat eggs or cream. As mentioned in making macaron batter (page 23), this mixer will let you select from fast, medium, and slow speeds.

Citrus juicer

This citrus juicer, or citrus press, is used for making lemon curd. If you don't have a juicer, you can cut a lemon in half and squeeze it with your hands.

Plastic wrap

This is used to seal custard cream for storage. When storing it, you may want to write the name of the cream and the date it was made on the plastic wrap with a permanent marker.

How to Make Butter Cream #1

This vanilla-flavored butter cream is made from whole eggs. The recipe in this section is enough for about 45 macarons. The recipe on page 24 makes enough macaron batter for about 2 dozen macarons, so this recipe yields enough cream for 2 batches of pastries. You can freeze the unused cream or use it to make a variety of cream flavors. Refer to the samples on pages 44 to 45.

Ingredients (recommended volume: about 7 ounces/200 grams)

7 tablespoons (3.5 ounces/100 grams) unsalted butter
3 tablespoons (1.4 ounces/40 milliliters) water
3 tablespoons (1.4 ounces/40 grams) granulated sugar
1 egg
Vanilla extract

1.

Cut butter into pieces 0.2-inches/5-millimeters thick and place them in a heat-resistant bowl. Heat in the microwave oven (500W) for 10 seconds.

2.

Take the bowl out of the microwave oven and check the hardness of the butter. If the pieces are soft enough for your finger to press into them, the butter is done. If they are still hard, heat them for another 5 seconds.

Pointer:

Never melt butter in the microwave oven.

3.

Stir the butter with a spatula until it becomes smooth and creamy like mayonnaise.

4.

Put water and granulated sugar in a heat-resistant container and stir them well.

5.

Heat this mixture in microwave oven for 1 minute. Take the container out of the microwave and mix the water and sugar until the sugar is completely dissolved. Heat for another 4 minutes. Take the container out of the microwave and stir the mixture with a spoon.

Pointer:

Wear oven mitts or gloves during this process because the container can become very hot when heated.

6.

Scoop some syrup with a spoon and drop it into a small amount of water. Then try to scoop the syrup out of the water and make a ball with it using your fingers. If you can do this, the syrup has the right density.

7.

While heating the syrup, break an egg in a bowl and beat it lightly with a hand mixer. Pour the syrup made in step 6, like a thread, into the bowl and beat it at a high speed. Reduce the speed to medium and then to slow, and continue beating until the bottom of the bowl is no longer hot, and the mixture becomes white and heavy.

Pointer:

Place a wet cloth under the bowl so that it does not move when you beat the cream.

8.

Divide the butter prepared in step 3, adding it to the syrup in two or three batches. Beat with a hand mixer at medium speed each time you add the butter. When the butter is well mixed, the process is done.

Pointer:

While beating the butter and syrup, bubbles may appear that seem to separate the butter from the syrup. You may think you have made a mistake but just continue beating until the butter becomes creamy.

9.

Stir a drop or two of vanilla extract into the mixture. When the mixture is well stirred, it is done. Spread the cream between the puffs you made on pages 24 to 35. Now the macarons are ready to eat!

10.

Wrap the remainder of the cream with plastic wrap and place it in the freezer for future use. Write a date on the package to remind you when you made it. It can be kept frozen for at least one month.

HOW TO SANDWICH THE CREAM

Use a pastry bag to place some cream on the flat side of the macaron puff.

Cover the bottom puff (spread with cream) with another puff, with the flat sides facing in. Gently press the top puff into place so that the cream does not come out. The macaron is done!

ADDING VARIOUS FLAVORS TO BUTTER CREAM #1

Standard Vanilla Cream
The standard butter cream has a slight aroma of vanilla.

CREAMS WITH DRINK FLAVORS

Coffee Cream
Dissolve 2 tablespoons of instant coffee powder into the same amount of hot water.

Matcha Cream (green tea)
Knead 1 teaspoon (0.2 ounce/5 grams) matcha powder with 1 tablspoon of hot water.

CREAMS WITH JAM

Orange Jam Cream
3½ tablespoons (1.8 ounces/50 grams) orange jam or marmalade

Framboise Jam Cream
3½ tablespoons (1.8 ounces/50 grams) raspberry jam

CREAMS WITH ALCOHOL FLAVORS

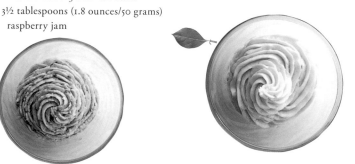

Blueberry Jam Cream
3½ tablespoons (1.8ounces/50 grams) blueberry jam

Grand Marnier Cream
1 or 2 tablespoons of Grand Marnier This is an orange liqueur with a citrus fragrance.

Kiwi Jam Cream
3½ tablespoons (1.8 ounces/50 grams) kiwifruit jam

Kirsch Cream
1 or 2 tablespoons of Kirsch (Kirsch eau de vie) This has a cherry brandy flavor.

Rum Cream
1 or 2 tablespoons of rum (Rhum Negri

Instead of adding vanilla cream as shown in the section How to Make Butter Cream #1 (see step 9, page 43), add the ingredients below. Cream can be refrigerated for two to three weeks. When you want to use it, whisk it before using. Even if the cream separates as you stir it, it will become creamy. Purée and other ingredients that have plenty of moisture tend to separate, so stir the cream well before squeezing it onto the macaron puff.

TYPES OF PURÉE CREAM

TYPES OF FLOWER WATER–FLAVORED CREAM

Orange Flower Water–Flavored Cream
1 tablespoon orange flower water
This adds a soft citrus fragrance.

Mango Cream
3 tablespoons (2.5 ounces/70 grams)
  mango purée

Passion Fruit Cream
3½ tablespoons (1.8 ounces/50 grams)
  passion fruit
This is a sweet-and-sour fruit with a
refreshing taste

Honey Cream
1 or 2 tablespoons of honey

Framboise Cream (raspberry)
4 tablespoons (2.8 ounces/80 grams)
  framboise purée
This has a sour taste.

Rose Water–Flavored Cream
1 tablespoon rose water
This adds a sweet rose fragrance.

Sesame Paste Cream
1 tablespoon white
  sesame-seed paste

Praline Cream
3½ tablespoons (1.8 ounces/50 grams)
  praline
This is a hazelnut or almond paste with
cocoa butter.

Caramel Cream
½ teaspoon caramel coloring

How to Make Butter Cream #2 (Black Tea Flavor)

This butter cream is made from two egg yolks. The egg whites can be used for making macaron batter, or you can put them in a food storage bag and freeze them.

Ingredients

7 tablespoons (3.5 ounces/100 grams unsalted butter)
3½ tablespoons (1.7 ounces/50 milliliters milk)
1 teaspoon (0.1 ounces/3 grams) black tea (Earl Grey)
2 egg yolks
¼ cup (1.4 ounces/40 grams) granulated sugar

1.

Cut butter into pieces 0.2-inch/5-millimeters thick and place them in a heat-resistant bowl. Heat in the microwave oven for 5 seconds until pieces are soft enough for your finger to press into them. Knead the butter with a spatula until it becomes smooth and creamy like mayonnaise.

Pointer:

Never melt the butter in the microwave oven!

2.

Pour milk in a pot and boil. Turn off the heat, add black tea to it, and cover the mixture with a lid to steam for about 10 minutes.

Note:

If you want to add a fresh mint flavor, almond slices, or shredded coconut, add any of these flavors with the black tea.

3.

Break the egg yolks in a bowl, whisk, and then add the granulated sugar. Stir until the egg appears white.

4.

Add the milk prepared in step 2 into the bowl used in step 3. Pour the mixture back into the pot, straining it with a strainer. Press the tea leaves with a spatula to squeeze out the flavor.

5.

Simmer until the mixture is thick and creamy.

6.

Pour the mixture prepared in step 5 into a bowl and beat it with a hand mixer at medium speed until it cools down and becomes heavy. When the mixture is hard enough that you can draw a line on it when scooped on a spatula, it is done.

7.

Divide the butter from step 1, adding it into the bowl in two or three batches. Blend with a hand mixer. When the mixture is smooth, it is done.

To make the following variations, add the additional ingredients into the mixture during step 2 of the butter cream–making process.

Almond Cream
7 tablespoons (3.4 ounces/
100 milliliters) milk
3½ tablespoons (1.8 ounces/
50 grams) sliced almonds

Mint Cream
1/2 tablespoon
(0.4 ounces/10 grams) fresh mint

Coconut Cream
7 tablespoons
(3.4 ounces/100 milliliters) milk
2 tablespoons (1.1 ounces/30 grams)
shredded coconut

Note: You can dry the almond slices or shredded coconut in the oven and use it in baking cookies, and other treats.

Using the Butter Cream Stored in the Refrigerator

If the butter cream stored in the refrigerator becomes too hard to be squeezed out later from a pastry bag, thaw it at room temperature and stir with an whisk or a hand mixer. It may separate while you stir it, but just continue stirring. Eventually it will become creamy. Purées and other ingredients have plenty of moisture that can separate easily. Be sure to stir the cream before squeezing it on the macaron puffs.

How to Make Custard Cream (Vanilla Flavor)

Custard cream is made from a custard base of flour, eggs, milk, and sugar boiled down to make a thick cream. You can use it not only in macarons but also in cream puffs and other custard pastries.

Ingredients

¼ vanilla bean
2 egg yolks
¼ cup (1.8 ounces/50 grams) granulated sugar
⅓ cup (0.5 ounce/15 grams) pastry flour
⅞ cup (6.8 ounces/200 milliliters) milk

1.

Slice a vanilla bean pod lengthwise and scrape out the seeds with the back of the knife. If you do not have vanilla beans, use 2 to 3 drops of vanilla extract.

2.

Put the egg yolks in a bowl and add granulated sugar. Whisk until the mixture appears slightly white.

3.

Add pastry flour and mix it lightly.

4.

Put milk and vanilla bean pods in a pot and warm it. While stirring the mixture, pour the milk into the bowl used in step 3.

VARIATIONS OF CUSTARD CREAM

Lemon Custard Cream

This type of cream has a slight sour taste. In step 6 below, add 2 tablespoons of lemon juice before turning off the heat.
Note: Do not use vanilla beans for this flavor.

Cocoa Custard Cream

This type of cream has a chocolate flavor. Mince 1.4 ounces/40 grams of chocolate in advance and add it in step 6 before removing from heat.
Note: Do not use vanilla beans for this flavor.

5.

Pour the mixture back into the pot, straining it with a strainer.

6.

Heat on medium and stir with a spatula. When the mixture starts to bubble, stir for 1 minute and then turn off the heat.

7.

Spread the mixture in a square pan and cover with plastic wrap.

8.

Place the pan in ice water to cool down quickly. Put it in the refrigerator to keep it fresh until you are ready to use it. Before using it, smooth the top with a spatula.

How to Make Ganache

Ganache is made from a mixture of a chocolate base and whipping cream. This book presents three types of chocolate ganache: rich and sweet white, mild sweet, and bitter.

Rich and Sweet
White Ganache

Mild Sweet Ganache

Bitter Ganache

Ingredients

⅖ cup (3.4 ounces/100 milliliters) whipping cream
1 bar (3.5 ounces/100 grams) white, semi-sweet or bittersweet chocolate, finely chopped

1.

Put whipping cream in a pot and bring it to boil.

2.

Put chocolate in a bowl and add the cream from step 1.

3.

Mix slowly with a whisk. Stir about 100 times until it becomes glossy.

4.

Cool the mixture to room temperature. Then put it in an airtight container and store it in the refrigerator. When ready to use, warm it up in a double boiler to soften it.

How to Make Chestnut Cream

This rich cream is made from butter and chestnut cream. Simply mix ingredients to make this cream.

Ingredients

4 tablespoons (1.8 ounces/50 grams) unsalted butter
3½ tablespoons (1.8 ounces/50 grams) canned chestnut cream
1 tablespoon rum (optional)

1.

Put butter in a bowl and knead it until it softens. Add chestnut cream and mix. Add rum as desired.

How to Make Caramel Cream

Caramel cream is made from water and sugar boiled down, thickened, and then mixed with whipping cream. The key for a tasty caramel is the way you cook it—the darker the color, the more bitter the taste becomes.

Ingredients

7 tablespoons (3.4 ounces/100 milliliters) whipping cream
½ cup (3.5 ounces/100 grams) granulated sugar
3½ tablespoons (1.7 ounces/50 milliliters) water

1.

Put whipping cream in a pot and warm it on the stove. Put granulated sugar and water in another pot and heat on medium. Shake the pot to dissolve the sugar. When the mixture turns to a caramel color, it is done.

2.

Remove caramel from heat, add the whipping cream, and mix well. When the mixture cools to room temperature, the caramel cream is done.

How to Make Lemon Curd

Lemon curd is a cream made from egg yolk, sugar, lemon juice, lemon peel, and cornstarch. The taste of lemon adds a refreshing flavor.

Ingredients

¼ cup (0.7 ounces/20 grams) cornstarch
¼ cup (1.8 ounces/50 grams) granulated sugar
3½ tablespoons (1.7 ounces/50 milliliters) water
1 egg yolk
2 tablespoons lemon juice
Peel from ½ lemon, minced

1.

Put cornstarch and granulated sugar into a pot and mix with a small whisk.

2.

When ingredients are mixed well, add water and stir.

3.

Heat on low and stir with a spatula until the mixture is transparent.

4.

Remove it from heat. Add an egg yolk and mix lightly.

5.

Add the lemon juice and lemon peel and mix. The lemon curd is done.

SERVING DRINKS WITH MACARONS

Macarons are a very sweet dessert, so serving them with a drink brings out a refreshing taste that stays in your mouth. And the drinks may tempt you to eat more delicious macarons! Below are three popular drinks that can be served with macarons.

Espresso

A small macaron goes well with a cup of espresso or other favorite coffee drink. Enjoy eating macarons in a cool ambience.

Herb Tea

Pour hot water over fresh mint leaves or other herbs, such as spearmint or peppermint. The mint's refreshing scent and the macaron's sweet taste combine for an exquisite harmony in your mouth.

Matcha (green tea)

This is a combination of the West (macaron) and the East (green tea). It may seem an odd duo, but the bittersweet taste of green tea brings out the macaron's sweetness.

Part 3

COMBINING ASSORTED PUFFS AND CREAMS

Now that you have learned how to make macaron puffs and creams, you have reached the final stage of making macarons: putting the puffs and creams together. Sandwich your favorite cream between your favorite puffs, and you are ready to eat your macarons!

Bon appétit! Choosing the puff and cream combinations is up to you. This section presents some of the popular combinations, showing two variations for each type of puff.

Sandwiched Puffs and Creams with Almond Powder Flavor

Vanilla

Framboise (raspberry) Cream   Peanut Cream

Caramel

Caramel Cream   Pastry Cream

Purple Yam

Chestnut Cream   Vanilla Cream

Chocolate

Sweet Ganache   Mango Cream

Matcha (green tea)

Red Bean Paste   Matcha Cream

Pistachio

Framboise (raspberry) Cream   Bitter Ganache

Sesame

Sesame Paste Cream

White Ganache

Coconut

Orange Jam Cream

Rum Cream

Framboise (raspberry)

Framboise (raspberry) Cream

White Ganache

Hazelnut

Praline Cream   Almond Cream

Café

Grand Marnier Cream   Coffee Cream

Tea

Black Tea Cream   Honey Cream

Sandwiched Puffs and Creams with Meringue Flavor

Rose

Rose Water–Flavored Cream   Lemon Curd

Red

Framboise (raspberry) Jam Cream   Kirsch Cream

Cassis

Bitter Ganache   Blueberry Jam Cream

Blue   Mint Cream   Lemon Custard Cream

Yellow-Green   Mango Cream   Vanilla Custard Cream

Yellow

Kiwi Jam Cream

Passion Fruit Cream

Orange

Orange Jam Cream

Orange Water–Flavored Cream

Caramel

Almond Cream

Caramel Cream

À la Carte: Petit Macaron Pastries

Here are three different kinds of small pastries using macaron puffs. Large puffs, however, add a gorgeous appeal to your table presentation and make your macarons look delicious. To make big macarons, squeeze out more paste than you would normally do for regular-sized macarons but follow the same baking procedure for the puffs.

Mont Blanc Macaron Pastry (left)

Sandwich praline cream (page 45) and fruits sprinkled in liquor between two plain puffs (page 24). On top, squeeze the praline cream out of the pastry bag using a star-shaped tip and making clockwise circles to create a Mont Blanc–like image.

Raspberry Macaron Pastry (center)

Sandwich Butter Cream #1 (page 42) and raspberries between two red-colored puffs (page 34) and then decorate the top with a raspberry. This pastry has a charming color combination and, between the sweet macaron and the sweet-and-sour raspberries,

offers an exquisite harmony of taste.

Chestnut Macaron Pastry (right)

Squeeze out Butter Cream #1 (page 42) on a chocolate puff (page 32) and then decorate with chestnuts cooked in sweet syrup and roasted walnuts. Finally, sprinkle cocoa powder on the pastry using a tea strainer. This is a small but richly filled macaron pastry.

Part 4

GIFT WRAPPING IDEAS FOR MACARONS

Small, round, and colorful macarons are really cute. They make the best gifts and delight anyone who receives them. This section presents some easy-to-do wrapping ideas for your macarons. Make your own stylish gift for your special one.

CLEAR PLASTIC BOX

Put two macarons in a clear plastic box. With a box like this, you won't have to worry about the cream dripping out of the puffs.

Letter with a Macaron

Place a macaron inside an envelope with your letter in it. A heart-shaped macaron sends a love message. There is no doubt that your heart will be accepted by your special someone! To make a heart-shaped macaron, pipe out the batter to form two overlapping circles.

ROUND BOX

Place a round macaron inside a round box and tie a cute ribbon around it. Your friend will be excited to find a charming macaron popping out of the box.

BAKING PAPER WRAP

Wrap each macaron in baking paper and close it with a decorative wire. Using a wire topped with a flower decoration makes your macaron gift look sophisticated. If you do not have decorated wire, you can attach a fresh flower.

CREAM JAR ASSORTMENT

Gather an assortment of macarons and add a jar of butter cream. Wrap them in a waxed paper bag and include a wooden cream spreader. A friend will have fun spreading the butter cream on his or her favorite macaron!

Transparent Bag

Put colorful macarons inside a transparent waxed paper bag. The macarons look cute and colorful peeping through the bag.

Part 5

Easy-to-Make Desserts Using Leftover Egg Yolks

Macaron puffs are made from egg whites, so the yolks are not used. This section presents six popular desserts that are made from egg yolks instead of whole eggs. The recipes are not difficult to do, so make sure to try them. You never have to waste eggs again!

RICH AND CREAMY PUDDING

Both children and adults love this rich, vanilla-flavored pudding. It may look like regular pudding, but when you stick a spoon into it, you will discover its decadent and creamy taste.

INGREDIENTS (fills four pudding molds, 2 inches/ 5 centimeters in diameter)

3 egg yolks
⅛ cup (1.1 ounces/30 grams) granulated sugar
6 tablespoons (3.4 ounces/ 100 cc) whipping cream
6 tablespoons (3.4 ounces/ 100 cc) milk
1 vanilla bean
1 teaspoon to 1 tablespoon liqueur (rum, Grand Marnier, or your favorite liqueur)

1.

Put the egg yolks in a bowl and add granulated sugar. Stir until the mixture begins to lighten in color. Add whipping cream and milk and stir again.

2.

Slit the vanilla bean pod and scrape out the seeds. Add them and the liqueur into the bowl in step 1.

3.

Pour the mixture made in step 2 into the pudding molds. Put the molds in a bain-marie and bake at 300°F (150°C) for about 40 minutes. When the mixture firms and the center of the surface shakes, you can take it out from the bain-marie.

ICEBOX COOKIES

These cookies look bulky but are made with little sugar.
You can bake many cookies using only 2 egg yolks. Try
making vanilla, chocolate, and marble flavors.

INGREDIENTS (makes about 40 cookies, 1.6 inches/
  4 centimeters in diameter)

Vanilla Flavor

¾ cup (5.3 ounces/150 grams) unsalted butter
½ cup (3.5 ounces/100 grams) granulated sugar
2 egg yolks
2¼ cups (8.8 ounces/250 grams) pastry flour
Vanilla extract

Chocolate Flavor

¾ cup (5.3 ounces/150 grams) unsalted butter
½ cup (3.5 ounces/100 grams) granulated sugar
2 egg yolks
2 cups (7 ounces/200 grams) pastry flour
½ cup (1.8 ounces/50 grams) cocoa (optional)

1.

Slice the butter into pieces 2-inches/
5-centimeters thick and put them in a
heat-resistant bowl. Warm in the microwave oven (500W). Continue heating for
10 seconds until the butter pieces are soft
enough for your finger to press into them.

2.

When the butter becomes soft and creamy
like mayonnaise, add the granulated sugar
and whisk until the mixture appears white.

3.

Add the egg yolks and stir well. Then, add
pastry flour while sifting it. (For chocolate
flavor, mix cocoa with the pastry flour
in advance.) Add a few drops of vanilla
extract to give some fragrance.

4.

The mixture should no longer be powdery.
Put it in the refrigerator until the batter
becomes firm.

5.

Roll the dough into a log about
1.6 inches/4 centimeters in diameter.
Wrap it with plastic wrap and put it in
the refrigerator until it becomes firm.

6.

When the dough becomes hard, cut it into
slices about 0.3-inches/8-millimeters thick.
Bake them in the oven at 350°F (180°C) for
10 to 12 minutes.

Note: To create marble cookies, use equal
amounts of vanilla dough and chocolate
dough and roll them together.

CARAMEL ICE CREAM

This ice cream has a bitter caramel taste. The secret to maintaining its smooth texture is to repeat the sequence of freezing and stirring several times.

INGREDIENTS (for one airtight container, 7.1 by 3.9 inches/18 by 10 centimeters)

3½ tablespoons (1.7 ounces/50 milliliters) whipping cream
1¼ cups (10.1 ounces/300 milliliters) milk
1 tablespoon water
½ cup (3.2 ounces/90 grams) granulated sugar
3 egg yolks

1.

Put the whipping cream and milk in a pot and warm it up.

2.

In another pot, combine the water and ¼ cup (1.8 ounces/50 grams) of the sugar. Heat until it bubbles and darkens to a deep golden color. Remove from heat and immediately add the cream prepared in step 1 and then stir. When the mixture forms lumps, put it on low heat and stir until smooth.

3.

Put the egg yolks and the remaining sugar in a bowl, and whisk until it appears white. Add the mixture made in step 2 to this and pour the combined mixture back into the pot, straining it through a strainer. Turn heat to medium and stir with a spatula until the mixture is thick and creamy. To test for doneness, scoop a small amount of the mixture out of the pot with a spatula. You should be able to draw a line through it using your finger.

4.

Pour contents of the pot back into the bowl from step 3. Float the bowl in ice water to cool. When it has cooled, put the mixture in a container and store it in the refrigerator.

5.

When the mixture becomes firm, put it back in a bowl and stir it with a whisk to smooth it. Put it in a container again and freeze it. Repeat this sequence several times.

CRÈME BRÛLÉE

Crème brûlée consists of thick cream topped with a crisp surface of caramelized sugar. The bitter taste of the caramel is particularly appealing to adults.

INGREDIENTS (for 5 cocotte molds, 2 inches/ 5 centimeters in diameter)

½ cup (3.4 ounces/100 milliliters) whipping cream
½ cup (3.4 ounces/100 milliliters) milk
¼ vanilla bean
2 egg yolks
1 tablespoon (0.4 ounce/10 grams) granulated sugar, plus more for topping
1 tablespoon rum or Grand Marnier (optional)

1.

Put the whipping cream and milk in a pot. Scrape the vanilla seeds out of the pod and put the entire vanilla pod into the pot. Heat until the cream starts to bubble around the edge of the pot.

2.

Put the egg yolks in a bowl and add the 1 tablespoon (0.4 ounce/10 grams) granulated sugar. Whisk until the mixture appears white.

3.

Pour the cream from step 1 into the mixture made in step 2. Add the rum (if using) and pour through a fine-mesh strainer into a bowl.

4.

Pour the mixture into a heat-resistant container. Put it in a water bath and bake in the oven at 300°F (150°C) for about 30 minutes.

5.

Once the custard is baked, sprinkle granulated sugar over the top while smoothing the surface. Burn the sugary surface with a kitchen torch. (If you do not have a kitchen torch, you can use the broiler.)

Bavarian Cream

Plain Bavarian cream is delicious, but you can enrich its taste more by pouring purée over it. It has a sweet taste and thick texture that melts on your tongue.

INGREDIENTS (for 5 to 6 molds, 2.8 inches/ 7 centimeters in diameter)

1 envelope (0.2 ounce/6 grams) gelatin
⅞ cup (6.8 ounces/200 milliliters) milk
¼ vanilla bean
3 egg yolks
¼ cup (1.8 ounces/50 grams) granulated sugar
⅜ cup (3.4 ounces/100 milliliters) whipping cream
Mango and raspberry purée

1.

Combine gelatin with 2 tablespoons water. Put the milk, vanilla seeds (scraped out of the bean), and the vanilla bean pod in a pot and heat them to the boiling point.

2.

Put the egg yolks and granulated sugar in a bowl, and whisk them until the mixture lightens in color. Add the milk from step 1 and then put the whole mixture back into the pot, straining it as you do. Heat, stirring with a spatula, until the mixture becomes thick and creamy. To test for doneness, scoop a little liquid from the pot with a spatula; you should be able to draw a line in it with your finger.

3.

Turn off heat and add the gelatin and water mixture. Stir. Put mixture into a bowl and cool bowl in ice water until liquid sets.

4.

Put the whipping cream in another bowl and whisk firmly until traces of the whisk remain on the cream.

5.

Combine the mixtures from steps 3 and 4 and pour cream into molds. Cool in refrigerator until firm.

6.

Pour a topping purée over cream before serving.

Banana Shake

Banana shakes probably remind you of a taste from the good ol' days. The nutritional value is increased with the combination of bananas, egg yolks, and milk, so one glass is enough to drink for a quick breakfast.

INGREDIENTS (makes one glass)

1 egg yolk
1 teaspoon granulated sugar (more or less to taste)
⅜ cup (3.4 ounces/100 milliliters) milk
½ banana
2 to 3 ice cubes

1.

Put all the ingredients in a blender. Blend well and then pour into a glass.

Note: You can use strawberries or chocolate syrup instead of bananas to make this sweet and tasty shake.